CONGRATUL[...]

FOR GIVING A SHIT! IT'S TIME TO RECLAIM ALL OF YOUR INNER AWESOMENESS THAT HAS BEEN FORGOTTEN OR FLUSHED AWAY OVER THE YEARS. YOU ARE ON THE JOURNEY OF BECOMING THE BEST VERSION OF YOU...

A PORCELAIN GOD!

LET'S EXAMINE YOUR INTERNAL PLUMBING & LEARN HOW TO POTTY LIKE A ROCKSTAR!

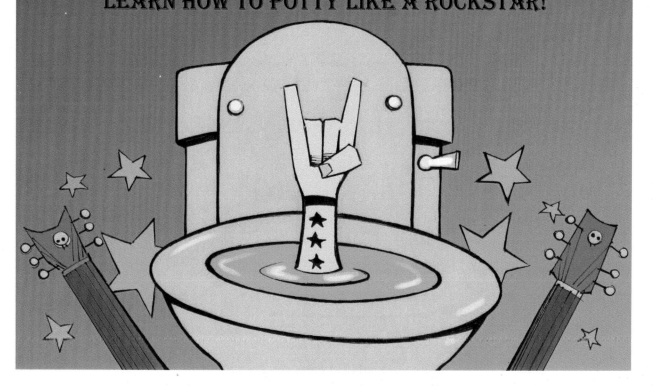

MAKING CHANGE & TRANSFORMATION is EXCITING AND WILL CAUSE YOU TO STEP OUTSIDE OF YOUR COMFORT ZONE.
YOU ARE BEGINNING A JOURNEY INTO THE UNKNOWN.
EMBARKING ON A PATH TOWARDS A LIFE OF SELF DISCOVERY & FREEDOM...
THE TP TRAIL!

YOU CANNOT FAIL ON THE TP TRAIL!

What Porcelain Throne Do You Claim as Your Own?

You're here to create & fulfill your DREAMS. You are a limitless being in a limitless world!

Who do you want to become? What do you want to do?

Decide on the DREAM that fulfills your SOUL, its like the water in your toilet bowl!

LIFE IS FILLED WITH OPPORTUNITY & CHOICES. YOU AT ANY MOMENT CAN MAKE A CONSCIOUS DECISION TO CHANGE YOURSELF & THE TRAJECTORY OF YOUR PATH! OPENING YOUR MIND, ACCEPTING YOUR WORTHINESS & BELIEVING IN YOURSELF IS THE START OF THE JOURNEY!

YOU CAN ONLY RECEIVE WHAT YOU BELIEVE!

CREATE A ROADMAP OF HOW YOU WILL GET TO THE GOLDEN THRONE...THE TOILET OF YOUR DREAMS IS EASIER THAN IT SEEMS!

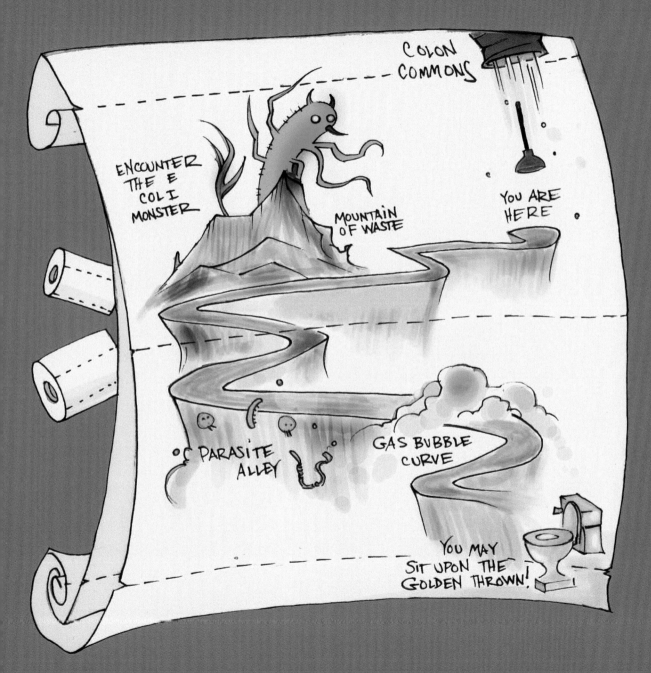

YOU HAVE ESTABLISHED A
DREAM & A MAP,
NOW HOW THE HECK DO YOU
ACHIEVE THAT CRAP?

STARTS WITH YOU!

JOURNEY WITHIN YOURSELF TO SEE
WHAT YOUR TOILET HOLDS,
USUALLY A VERY DIRTY BOWL!

STAY SANE ELIMINATE TOILET BRAIN...

YOUR thoughts CREATE your REALITY!
IT IS IMPORTANT TO KEEP YOUR MIND AS CRYSTAL CLEAR AS POSSIBLE.

A CLEAN BOWL IS YOUR GOAL!

SOME EXPERTS SAY THAT YOU PROCESS UP TO 70,000 THOUGHTS PER DAY.
THAT'S A SHIT TON OF BRAIN ACTIVITY!
NO WONDER IT'S EASY TO LOSE YOUR WAY.

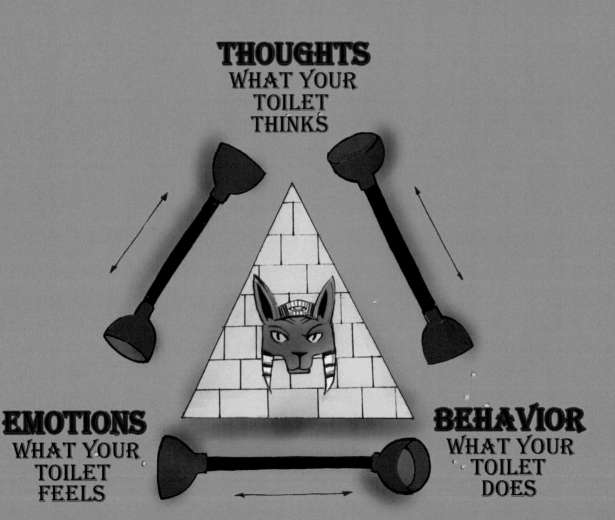

YOUR THOUGHTS PUT YOU ON THE POTS!

YOUR MIND DICTATES HOW YOU FEEL & WHAT YOU DO.
BY SHIFTING HOW YOU THINK
& RECOGNIZING THOSE NEGATIVE
SELF-SABOTAGING THOUGHTS
YOU HAVE THE ABILITY TO CHANGE YOUR BRAIN.

REPLACE THE UNPLEASANT THOUGHTS WITH ONES
THAT FEEL GOOD!

PLUNGE THE POO DOWN.
THERE'S A NEW BRAIN IN TOWN!

LIFE IS LIKE USING YOUR TOILET. TO KEEP BALANCE YOU MUST KEEP FLUSHING.

-ALBERT EINSTOOL

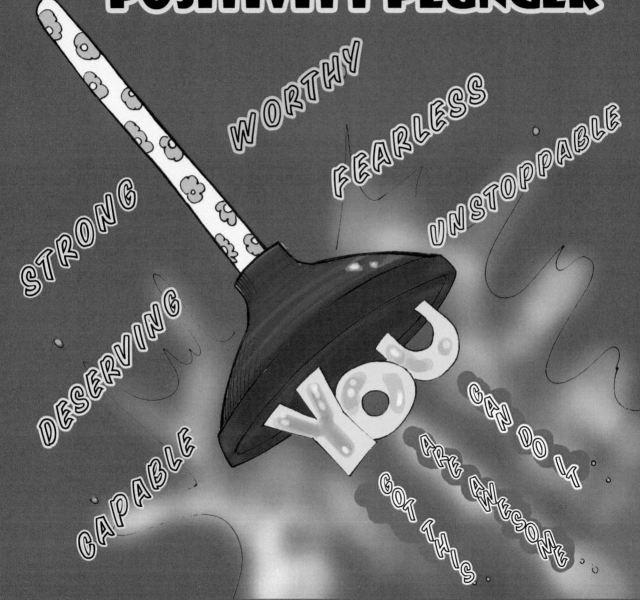

FLUSH THE SLUSH

NOTICE HOW YOU FEEL WHEN YOU'RE FILLED
WITH HAPPY THOUGHTS.
NOW, THINK ABOUT HOW YOU FEEL WHEN
YOUR BRAIN IS IN THE DRAIN.

THERE'S A BIG DIFFERENCE.

SO WHEN IT'S BROWN, FLUSH IT DOWN!

PULL OUT YOUR POSITIVITY PLUNGER
& YOUR TOILET WILL BE FREE OF DEBRIS &
YOU'LL BE AS HAPPY AS CAN BE!

THOUGHTS

SH... THOUGHT	TO	IT THOUGHT
I'M NOT ENOUGH...		I AM ENOUGH!
I'M NOT WANTED...		I AM LOVABLE!
I'M NOT SMART ENOUGH...		I AM SUPER SMART!
I CAN'T...		I CAN DO ANYTHING I PUT MY MIND TO!
I'M AFRAID OF FAILING...		I AM A SUCCESS!
I DON'T DESERVE IT...		I AM DESERVING OF SUCCESS!
I'M TOO OLD...		I AM THE PERFECT AGE TO ACHIEVE!
I DON'T HAVE THE TIME...		I AM ALWAYS ABLE TO MAKE TIME IN MY LIFE!

BECOME AWARE, DON'T DESPAIR

HERE'S THE TOILET TRUTH:

WE'RE ALL PROGRAMMED WITH
LIMITING, SELF SABOTAGING THOUGHTS. IT'S
PART OF WHAT MAKES US HUMAN.

EXCITING NEWS IS THEY ARE
UNTRUE & YOU HAVE THE POWER TO
SWAP YOUR THOUGHTS.

WHENEVER A SH... THOUGHT
STARTS TO BUBBLE,
REPLACE WITH AN IT THOUGHT
WITH NO TROUBLE!

DEALING WITH WHAT YOU'RE FEELING...

PAST	PRESENT	FUTURE
SADNESS ANGER REGRET	OPEN AWARE ALIVE	ANXIOUS NERVOUS FEAR
LET GO OF WHAT HAS ALREADY HAPPENED, USE IT AS INFORMATION TO HELP GUIDE YOU IN THE PRESENT MOMENT.	ALLOW YOURSELF TO FULLY RECEIVE THE MAGIC OF THE PRESENT MOMENT. IT'S THE ONLY THING THAT CURRENTLY EXISTS.	RELEASE THE NEED TO CONTROL THE UNKNOWN.
DEPRESSION	THE PLACE OF CHANGE & TRANSFORMATION	ANXIETY

IT'S HEALTHY TO EXPERIENCE ALL OF THESE EMOTIONS!

SOCIETY TEACHES YOU THAT IF YOU'RE DEPRESSED OR ANXIOUS THAT THERE IS SOMETHING WRONG WITH YOU BUT WHAT IF THAT IS UNTRUE?
WHAT IF YOU ARE JUST STUCK IN POOPY PLUMBING?

LIVING IN THE PRESENT IS EFFERVESCENT!

INSANITY IS USING THE SAME CLOGGED TOILET OVER &OVER AGAIN & EXPECTING IT NOT TO STINK!

-ALBERT EINSTOOL

INTRODUCING...
THE POO INSIDE OF YOU

LIMITING BELIEFS   **FEAR**   **EXCUSES**

LIMITING BELIEFS

ARE THE LIES YOU TELL YOURSELF
THAT HOLD YOU BACK
FROM YOUR FULL POTENTIAL!
THEY ARE CREATED THROUGH CHILDHOOD,
OTHER PEOPLE & EXPERIENCES!
GET SOME RELIEF,FLUSH
YOUR LIMITING BELIEF !

FEAR

IS DESIGNED TO STOP YOU & IS
FALSE EVIDENCE APPEARING REAL.
YOUR DREAMS WILL CAUSE FEAR...
YOU HAVE THE TOOLS
TO CLEAN YOUR REAR!

EXCUSES

ARE WHAT YOU USE TO JUSTIFY
UNMET GOALS.
OUR WAY TO DEFLECT BLAME
& NOT TAKE OWNERSHIP.

THERE IS NO EXCUSE, FOR NOT WIPING YOUR CABOOSE!

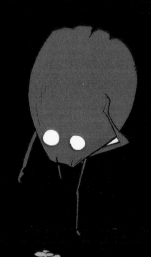

A TOILET IS A PART OF A WHOLE CALLED BY "US" THE BATHROOM.

- ALBERT EINSTOOL

SHIT HAPPENS, ROLL WITH IT!

LIFE'S FULL OF UNEXPECTED SURPRISES. UPS, DOWNS & ALL - AROUNDS.

"UNCONTROLLABLE SITUATIONS"

LEARN TO BE WITH WHAT IS.

HOLD YOUR ROLL, CAUSE YOU'RE IN CONTROL!

IT'S IMPORTANT TO TAKE OWNERSHIP OF YOUR EMOTIONS & UNDERSTAND THE DIFFERENCE BETWEEN REACTING & RESPONDING!

REACT:

ACT INSTANTANEOUSLY & DEFENSIVELY BECAUSE YOU'RE UNCOMFORTABLE WITH WHAT IS HAPPENING!
"LOSING YOUR SHIT"

RESPOND:

ACT IN A CAREFUL & CONTROLLED MANNER BECAUSE YOU'RE USING REASON & LOGIC.
"OWNING YOUR SHIT"

SILENCE YOUR MIND
CREATE TOILET TIME!

ONE OF THE GREATEST GIFTS YOU CAN
GIVE YOURSELF IS
SILENCE & STILLNESS.

PROBLEMS RESOLVE,
WORRYING DISAPPEARS &
LIFE BECOMES CRYSTAL CLEAR!

LETTING GO... IS HOW YOU GROW!

FLUSH THE IMAGE OF WHO YOU THINK
YOU SHOULD BE FOR OTHERS &
EMBRACE ALL THAT YOU CAN BE
FOR YOU !

STOP LIVING UP TO OTHER PEOPLE'S
EXPECTATIONS OF WHO YOU
SHOULD BE & HOW YOU SHOULD ACT.

LET GO OF YOUR NEED TO PLEASE.
FIND YOUR AUTHENTIC
SELF INSTEAD.

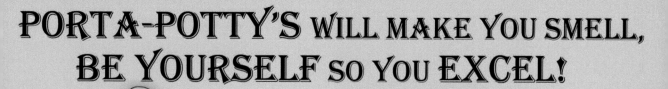

PORTA-POTTY'S WILL MAKE YOU SMELL,
BE YOURSELF SO YOU EXCEL!

YOUR AUTHENTIC SELF
IS WHO YOU ARE!

FITTING IN - YOU BECOME
WHO YOU ARE SURROUNDED
WITH FOR THE NEED TO BE
ACCEPTED, FEEL PART OF A
GROUP & BE LIKED
BY OTHERS.

FLUSH FITTING IN!

YOU ARE A FINE PIECE OF PORCELAIN... DON'T LET ANYONE TREAT YOU LIKE A PORTA-POTTY!

-KATIE GOYETTE

LOVE THE SHIT OUT OF YOURSELF!

CRAPPY INTO HAPPY!

YOUR PERSONAL POWER
IS YOUR STATE OF MIND &
SELF MASTERY! YOU HAVE
ALL THE KNOWLEDGE TO
MANAGE YOUR TOILET &
INTERNAL EMOTIONAL
PLUMBING.

HAPPY
DREAMER
FAITH
LIFE
IDEAS
GOOD
POSITIVE
POWER
EMPOWER
ENERGY
LIFE
IDEAS
UNIVERSE
UNITY
THOUGHTS
LIFE
ENERGY
EMPOWER
GOOD
DREAM
OPTIMISM

DO YOUR BEST TO KEEP IT FRESH.

LIFE IS EVER - CHANGING.

PEOPLE, PLACES & SITUATIONS
ARE GOING TO FLOW IN & OUT OF YOUR LIFE.
ALLOW WHAT DOES NOT SERVE YOUR
GREATEST GOOD TO BE FLUSHED AWAY.

THE UNIVERSE IS HERE TO HELP YOU
FILL YOUR SOUL!
IT'S THE SUPPORT SYSTEM THAT
GUIDES YOU TO YOUR GOAL!

CRAP RECAP:

*YOU ARE **AWESOME** & GIVE A SHIT!

*YOU HAVE THE POWER TO CHANGE & TRANSFORM.

*DREAM OF WHO YOU WANT TO BECOME!

*CREATE A ROADMAP.

*NOTICE HOW NEGATIVE THOUGHTS MAKE YOU FEEL.

Positivity

*PULL OUT YOUR POSITIVITY PLUNGER!

*SWAP THE SH... THOUGHTS FOR IT THOUGHTS.

*YOUR POO = LIMITING BELIEFS, FEAR & EXCUSES.

*FLUSH THEM!!!

*SHIT HAPPENS...ROLL WITH IT!

*CONTROL YOUR ROLL.

*OWN YOUR SHIT!

*GIVE YOURSELF THE GIFT OF SILENCE.
*LETTING GO IS HOW YOU GROW.
*FLUSH FITTING IN.
*LOVE YOUR AUTHENTIC SELF!
*TURN CRAPPY INTO HAPPY!

*BE ALL THE AWESOMENESS YOU WERE BORN TO BE.

*MOST IMPORTANTLY... BE YOU!

*LOVE WHO YOU ARE, AS YOU ARE, WHERE YOU ARE
  IN EVERY MOMENT.

*YOU ARE A WORK IN PROGRESS ON THE PATH TO
    BECOMING YOUR BEST SELF!